GOD'S
PROMISES
FOR
TODAY'S
BELIEVER

GOD'S PROMISES FOR TODAY'S BELIEVER

Ⓦ *Whitaker House*

GOD'S PROMISES FOR TODAY'S BELIEVER

ISBN: 0-88368-162-5
Printed in the United States of America
Copyright © 1997 by Whitaker House

Whitaker House
30 Hunt Valley Circle
New Kensington, PA 15068

7 8 9 10 11 12 13 14 15 16 / 06 05 04 03 02 01 00 99 98

Contents

God Promises Material Blessings............67

God's Promises When You Feel...............73

God's Promises in Times of.....................91

God's Promises for Those Who 106

God's Promises for Those Who Are 122

Introduction

The God we know through Christ Jesus is a God of promise. His promises are unmerited blessings. Some are conditional, some unexplainable, but all are a result of God's grace.

His promises are guaranteed through the total victory that Christ won for us. In Christ alone, we find fulfillment of each promise, and in Him we become recipients of His grace.

As a believer in Jesus Christ, you are a child of God and an heir to all His precious promises. Like any inheritance you might receive, you must acknowledge and claim these promises before they can become effective in your life.

This book contains God's will and testament to you. It lists your inheritance: the blessings and gifts you are entitled to as God's child.

A written will must sometimes be read repeatedly in order for a person to actually comprehend the significance of all that has been inherited. This is also true of God's Word. As you meditate on God's promises, the reality of all He wants to give you will saturate your spirit. This will give you confidence to believe and claim each promise as your own.

Some legal documents have qualifying clauses written in fine print. In the same way, some of God's promises have certain conditions that must be met before they will be granted. As you study each promise carefully, take note of any qualifying conditions. You may need to make some changes in your life in order to meet God's requirements and receive His blessings. But don't be discouraged. Your faithful Father has promised to help you and change you by His Spirit.

As a loving Father, God wants to give His children good things. He has left us an inheritance—a spiritual, physical, and personal treasury of blessings. When you reach out and claim what the Father has so lovingly provided for you, great joy fills His heart.

What do you need today? Healing, peace, protection, hope? Begin reading this book at your greatest point of need, and take hold of God's promises. Acknowledge them as your inheritance, claim them as your own, and receive them into your life.

God Promises to...

KEEP HIS PROMISES

1. *He who promised is faithful.*
                              (Hebrews 10:23 NIV)

2. *God, who called you to become his child, will do all this for you, just as he promised.*
                              (1 Thessalonians 5:24 TLB)

3. *God is not a man, that he should lie, nor a son of man, that he should change his mind. Does he speak and then not act? Does he promise and not fulfill?*
                              (Numbers 23:19 NIV)

4. *I have spoken it, I will also bring it to pass; I have purposed it, I will also do it.*
                              (Isaiah 46:11 KJV)

5. *What a God he is! How perfect in every way! All his promises prove true.*
                              (Psalm 18:30 TLB)

13

6. *I will never completely take away my loving-kindness from them, nor let my promise fail. No, I will not break my covenant; I will not take back one word of what I said.*
(Psalm 89:33–34 TLB)

7. *[Jesus Christ] carries out and fulfills all of God's promises, no matter how many of them there are; and we have told everyone how faithful he is, giving glory to his name.*
(2 Corinthians 1:20 TLB)

8. *The Lord is faithful to his promises. Blessed are all those who wait for him to help them.*
(Isaiah 30:18 TLB)

HEAR OUR PRAYERS

9. *The eyes of the Lord are on the righteous and his ears are attentive to their prayer.*
(1 Peter 3:12 NIV)

10. *Yes, the Lord hears the good man when he calls to him for help and saves him out of all his troubles.* (Psalm 34:17 TLB)

11. *This is the confidence that we have in him, that, if we ask any thing according to his will, he heareth us: and if we know that he hear us, whatsoever we ask, we know that*

we have the petitions that we desired of him.
(1 John 5:14–15 KJV)

12. *The Lord has set apart the redeemed for himself. Therefore he will listen to me and answer when I call to him.* (Psalm 4:3 TLB)

13. *He will listen to the prayers of the destitute, for he is never too busy to heed their requests.* (Psalm 102:17 TLB)

14. *Behold, the LORD'S hand is not shortened, that it cannot save; neither his ear heavy, that it cannot hear.* (Isaiah 59:1 KJV)

15. *If my people, who are called by my name, will humble themselves and pray and seek my face and turn from their wicked ways, then will I hear from heaven and will forgive their sin and will heal their land.*
(2 Chronicles 7:14 NIV)

ANSWER OUR PRAYERS

16. *Call unto me, and I will answer thee, and show thee great and mighty things, which thou knowest not.* (Jeremiah 33:3 KJV)

17. *I tell you, whatever you ask for in prayer, believe that you have received it, and it will be yours.* (Mark 11:24 NIV)

18. *I will answer them before they even call to me. While they are still talking to me about their needs, I will go ahead and answer their prayers!* (Isaiah 65:24 TLB)

19. *You will call, and the LORD will answer; you will cry for help, and he will say: Here am I.* (Isaiah 58:9 NIV)

20. *Until now you have not asked for anything in my name. Ask and you will receive, and your joy will be complete.* (John 16:24 NIV)

21. *If you remain in me and my words remain in you, ask whatever you wish, and it will be given you.* (John 15:7 NIV)

God Promises
Spiritual Blessings

SALVATION

22. *God did not send his Son into the world to condemn the world, but to save the world through him.* (John 3:17 NIV)

23. *And she shall bring forth a son, and thou shalt call his name JESUS: for he shall save his people from their sins.*

(Matthew 1:21 KJV)

24. *If thou shalt confess with thy mouth the Lord Jesus, and shalt believe in thine heart that God hath raised him from the dead, thou shalt be saved. For with the heart man believeth unto righteousness; and with the mouth confession is made unto salvation.*

(Romans 10:9–10 KJV)

25. *Anyone who calls upon the name of the Lord will be saved.* (Romans 10:13 TLB)

26. *It is by grace you have been saved, through faith—and this not from yourselves, it is the gift of God—not by works, so that no one can boast.* (Ephesians 2:8–9 NIV)

27. *God our Savior...wants all men to be saved and to come to a knowledge of the truth.* (1 Timothy 2:3–4 NIV)

28. *Now all those who flee to him to save them can take new courage when they hear such assurances from God; now they can know without doubt that he will give them the salvation he has promised them.* (Hebrews 6:18 TLB)

NEW LIFE

29. *We were therefore buried with him through baptism into death in order that, just as Christ was raised from the dead through the glory of the Father, we too may live a new life.* (Romans 6:4 NIV)

30. *Jesus said...“I have come that they may have life, and have it to the full.”* (John 10:7, 10 NIV)

31. *He personally carried the load of our sins in his own body when he died on the cross so that we can be finished with sin and live a good life from now on.* (1 Peter 2:24 TLB)

32. *When someone becomes a Christian, he becomes a brand new person inside. He is not the same anymore. A new life has begun!* (2 Corinthians 5:17 TLB)

33. *We…are being transformed into his likeness with ever-increasing glory, which comes from the Lord, who is the Spirit.* (2 Corinthians 3:18 NIV)

34. *I will give you a new heart—I will give you new and right desires—and put a new spirit within you. I will take out your stony hearts of sin and give you new hearts of love.* (Ezekiel 36:26 TLB)

35. *I have been crucified with Christ: and I myself no longer live, but Christ lives in me. And the real life I now have within this body is a result of my trusting in the Son of God, who loved me and gave himself for me.* (Galatians 2:20 TLB)

36. *The person who has been born into God's family does not make a practice of sinning because now God's life is in him; so he can't*

keep on sinning, for this new life has been born into him and controls him—he has been born again.   (1 John 3:9 TLB)

FREEDOM

37. *Sin need never again be your master, for now you are no longer tied to the law where sin enslaves you, but you are free under God's favor and mercy.*   (Romans 6:14 TLB)

38. *There is therefore now no condemnation to them which are in Christ Jesus, who walk not after the flesh, but after the Spirit. For the law of the Spirit of life in Christ Jesus hath made me free from the law of sin and death.*   (Romans 8:1–2 KJV)

39. *It is for freedom that Christ has set us free. Stand firm, then, and do not let yourselves be burdened again by a yoke of slavery.*
(Galatians 5:1 NIV)

40. *Everyone who trusts in him is freed from all guilt and declared righteous.*
(Acts 13:39 TLB)

41. *Now the Lord is the Spirit, and where the Spirit of the Lord is, there is freedom.*
(2 Corinthians 3:17 NIV)

42. *Now that you have been set free from sin and have become slaves to God, the benefit you reap leads to holiness, and the result is eternal life.* (Romans 6:22 NIV)

43. *If the Son sets you free, you will be free indeed.* (John 8:36 NIV)

FORGIVENESS

44. *What happiness for those whose guilt has been forgiven! What joys when sins are covered over! What relief for those who have confessed their sins and God has cleared their record.* (Psalm 32:1–2 TLB)

45. *Who dares accuse us whom God has chosen for his own? Will God? No! He is the one who has forgiven us and given us right standing with himself.* (Romans 8:33 TLB)

46. *In him we have redemption through his blood, the forgiveness of sins, in accordance with the riches of God's grace.*
(Ephesians 1:7 NIV)

47. *And all the prophets have written about him, saying that everyone who believes in him will have their sins forgiven through his name.* (Acts 10:43 TLB)

48. *I, even I, am he that blotteth out thy transgressions for mine own sake, and will not remember thy sins.* (Isaiah 43:25 KJV)

49. *Your sins have been forgiven in the name of Jesus our Savior.* (1 John 2:12 TLB)

50. *As far as the east is from the west, so far hath he removed our transgressions from us.* (Psalm 103:12 KJV)

51. *If we confess our sins, he is faithful and just to forgive us our sins, and to cleanse us from all unrighteousness.* (1 John 1:9 KJV)

52. *For he has rescued us out of the darkness and gloom of Satan's kingdom and brought us into the Kingdom of his dear Son, who bought our freedom with his blood and forgave us all our sins.*

(Colossians 1:13–14 TLB)

RIGHTEOUSNESS

53. *Now a righteousness from God, apart from law, has been made known, to which the Law and the Prophets testify. This righteousness from God comes through faith in Jesus Christ to all who believe.*

(Romans 3:21–22 NIV)

54. *God made him who had no sin to be sin for us, so that in him we might become the righteousness of God.* (2 Corinthians 5:21 NIV)

55. *Those who receive God's abundant provision of grace and of the gift of righteousness reign in life through the one man, Jesus Christ.* (Romans 5:17 NIV)

56. *It is because of him* [God] *that you are in Christ Jesus, who has become...our righteousness.* (1 Corinthians 1:30 NIV)

57. *For with the heart man believeth unto righteousness; and with the mouth confession is made unto salvation.*
(Romans 10:10 KJV)

58. *If Christ is in you, your body is dead because of sin, yet your spirit is alive because of righteousness.* (Romans 8:10 NIV)

59. *For the fruit of the Spirit is in all goodness and righteousness and truth.*
(Ephesians 5:9 KJV)

60. *When a man works, his wages are not credited to him as a gift, but as an obligation. However, to the man who does not work but trusts God who justifies the wicked, his faith is credited as righteousness.*
(Romans 4:4–5 NIV)

THE HOLY SPIRIT

61. *If even sinful persons like yourselves give children what they need, don't you realize that your heavenly Father will do at least as much, and give the Holy Spirit to those who ask for him?* (Luke 11:13 TLB)

62. *I will ask the Father and he will give you another Comforter, and he will never leave you. He is the Holy Spirit, the Spirit who leads into all truth.* (John 14:16–17 TLB)

63. *It is for your good that I am going away. Unless I go away, the Counselor will not come to you; but if I go, I will send him to you.* (John 16:7 NIV)

64. *You will receive power when the Holy Spirit comes on you; and you will be my witnesses...to the ends of the earth.*

(Acts 1:8 NIV)

65. *Because you are sons, God sent the Spirit of his Son into our hearts, the Spirit who calls out, "Abba, Father."*

(Galatians 4:6 NIV)

66. *Peter replied, "Repent and be baptized, every one of you, in the name of Jesus Christ for the forgiveness of your sins. And you will receive the gift of the Holy Spirit.*

The promise is for you and your children and for all who are far off—for all whom the Lord our God will call."

(Acts 2:38–39 NIV)

67. *He has put his own Holy Spirit into our hearts as a proof to us that we are living with him and he with us.*   (1 John 4:13 TLB)

68. *I will pour out my Spirit on your offspring, and my blessing on your descendants.*

(Isaiah 44:3 NIV)

HIS WORD

69. *Jesus answered, "It is written: 'Man does not live on bread alone, but on every word that comes from the mouth of God.'"*

(Matthew 4:4 NIV)

70. *For the word of God is living and active. Sharper than any double-edged sword, it penetrates even to dividing soul and spirit, joints and marrow; it judges the thoughts and attitudes of the heart.*

(Hebrews 4:12 NIV)

71. *My word...will not return to me empty, but will accomplish what I desire and achieve the purpose for which I sent it.*

(Isaiah 55:11 NIV)

72. *The whole Bible was given to us by inspiration from God and is useful to teach us what is true and to make us realize what is wrong in our lives; it straightens us out and helps us do what is right. It is God's way of making us well prepared at every point, fully equipped to do good to everyone.*
(2 Timothy 3:16–17 TLB)

73. *Your word, O LORD, is eternal; it stands firm in the heavens....Your laws endure to this day.* (Psalm 119:89, 91 NIV)

74. *The Word of the Lord will last forever. And his message is the Good News that was preached to you.* (1 Peter 1:25 TLB)

75. *The grass withers and the flowers fall, but the word of our God stands forever.*
(Isaiah 40:8 NIV)

DELIVERANCE FROM EVIL

76. *The LORD shall preserve thee from all evil: he shall preserve thy soul.* (Psalm 121:7 KJV)

77. *Yes, and the Lord will always deliver me from all evil and will bring me into his heavenly Kingdom. To God be the glory forever and ever.* (2 Timothy 4:18 TLB)

78. *The Lord is faithful; he will make you strong and guard you from satanic attacks of every kind.* (2 Thessalonians 3:3 TLB)

79. *Let those who love the LORD hate evil, for he guards the lives of his faithful ones and delivers them from the hand of the wicked.* (Psalm 97:10 NIV)

80. *[God] hath delivered us from the power of darkness, and hath translated us into the kingdom of his dear Son.* (Colossians 1:13 KJV)

81. *No one who has become part of God's family makes a practice of sinning, for Christ, God's Son, holds him securely, and the devil cannot get his hands on him.* (1 John 5:18 TLB)

82. *For I am persuaded that neither death, nor life, nor angels, nor principalities, nor powers, nor things present, nor things to come, nor height, nor depth, nor any other creature, shall be able to separate us from the love of God, which is in Christ Jesus our Lord.* (Romans 8:38–39 KJV)

83. *Because thou hast made the LORD, which is my refuge, even the most High, thy habitation; there shall no evil befall thee, neither*

shall any plague come nigh thy dwelling.
For he shall give his angels charge over
thee, to keep thee in all thy ways.

(Psalm 91:9–11 KJV)

HIS PRESENCE

84. *The LORD replied, "My Presence will go
with you, and I will give you rest."*

(Exodus 33:14 NIV)

85. *Look! I have been standing at the door, and
I am constantly knocking. If anyone hears
me calling him and opens the door, I will
come in and fellowship with him and he
with me.* (Revelation 3:20 TLB)

86. *If you love me, obey me; and I will ask the
Father and he will give you another Comforter, and he will never leave you.*

(John 14:15–16 TLB)

87. *For where two or three are gathered together in my name, there am I in the midst
of them.* (Matthew 18:20 KJV)

88. *Even though I walk through the valley of
the shadow of death, I will fear no evil, for
you are with me; your rod and your staff,
they comfort me.* (Psalm 23:4 NIV)

89. *I am with you always, even to the end of the world.*   (Matthew 28:20 TLB)

90. *Do not be afraid, for I am with you.*
                                   (Isaiah 43:5 NIV)

SPIRITUAL GROWTH

91. *As you sent me into the world, I am sending them into the world, and I consecrate myself to meet their need for growth in truth and holiness.*   (John 17:18–19 TLB)

92. *God who began the good work within you will keep right on helping you grow in his grace until his task within you is finally finished on that day when Jesus Christ returns.*   (Philippians 1:6 TLB)

93. *We, who with unveiled faces all reflect the Lord's glory, are being transformed into his likeness with ever-increasing glory, which comes from the Lord, who is the Spirit.*
                                (2 Corinthians 3:18 NIV)

94. *For as you know him better, he will give you, through his great power, everything you need for living a truly good life: he even shares his own glory and his own goodness with us!*   (2 Peter 1:3 TLB)

95. *You must learn to know God better and discover what he wants you to do....The more you go on in this way, the more you will grow strong spiritually and become fruitful and useful to our Lord Jesus Christ.*

(2 Peter 1:5, 8 TLB)

SPIRITUAL GIFTS

96. *See, I have...filled him with the Spirit of God, with skill, ability and knowledge in all kinds of crafts—to make artistic designs for work in gold, silver and bronze, to cut and set stones, to work in wood, and to engage in all kinds of craftsmanship.*

(Exodus 31:2–5 NIV)

97. *In Christ we who are many form one body, and each member belongs to all the others. We have different gifts, according to the grace given us. If a man's gift is prophesying, let him use it in proportion to his faith. If it is serving, let him serve; if it is teaching, let him teach; if it is encouraging, let him encourage; if it is contributing to the needs of others, let him give generously; if it is leadership, let him govern diligently; if it is showing mercy, let him do it cheerfully.*

(Romans 12:5–8 NIV)

98. *Now you have every grace and blessing;
    every spiritual gift and power for doing his
    will are yours during this time of waiting
    for the return of our Lord Jesus Christ.*
    (1 Corinthians 1:7 TLB)

99. *For God's gifts and his call can never be
    withdrawn; he will never go back on his
    promises.*
    (Romans 11:29 TLB)

TRUTH

100. *Since the Truth is in our hearts forever,
     God the Father and Jesus Christ his Son
     will bless us with great mercy and much
     peace, and with truth and love.*
     (2 John 1:2–3 TLB)

101. *For the fruit of the Spirit is in all goodness
     and righteousness and truth.*
     (Ephesians 5:9 KJV)

102. *Jesus said, "If you hold to my teaching,
     you are really my disciples. Then you will
     know the truth, and the truth will set you
     free."*
     (John 8:31–32 NIV)

103. *When we obey him, every path he guides us
     on is fragrant with his loving-kindness
     and his truth.*
     (Psalm 25:10 TLB)

104. *But when he, the Spirit of truth, comes, he will guide you into all truth. He will not speak on his own; he will speak only what he hears, and he will tell you what is yet to come.* (John 16:13 NIV)

105. *But I will send you the Comforter—the Holy Spirit, the source of all truth. He will come to you from the Father and will tell you all about me.* (John 15:26 TLB)

LOVE

106. *The LORD hath appeared of old unto me, saying, Yea, I have loved thee with an everlasting love: therefore with lovingkindness I have drawn thee.* (Jeremiah 31:3 KJV)

107. *"Though the mountains be shaken and the hills be removed, yet my unfailing love for you will not be shaken nor my covenant of peace be removed," says the LORD, who has compassion on you.* (Isaiah 54:10 NIV)

108. *For the Father himself loves you dearly because you love me and believe that I came from the Father.* (John 16:27 TLB)

109. *As the Father has loved me, so have I loved you.* (John 15:9 NIV)

110. *I will protect and bless him constantly and surround him with my love; he will be great because of me....I will love him forever and be kind to him always; my covenant with him will never end....I will never completely take away my lovingkindness from them, nor let my promise fail.* (Psalm 89:24, 28, 33 TLB)

111. *God demonstrates his own love for us in this: While we were still sinners, Christ died for us.* (Romans 5:8 NIV)

112. *God showed how much he loved us by sending his only Son into this wicked world to bring to us eternal life through his death. In this act we see what real love is: it is not our love for God but his love for us when he sent his Son to satisfy God's anger against our sins.* (1 John 4:9–10 TLB)

113. *If anyone acknowledges that Jesus is the Son of God, God lives in him and he in God. And so we know and rely on the love God has for us. God is love. Whoever lives in love lives in God, and God in him.*
(1 John 4:15–16 NIV)

114. *How great is the love the Father has lavished on us, that we should be called children of God!* (1 John 3:1 NIV)

JOY

115. *In thy presence is fulness of joy; at thy right hand there are pleasures for evermore.* (Psalm 16:11 KJV)

116. *These things have I spoken unto you, that my joy might remain in you, and that your joy might be full.* (John 15:11 KJV)

117. *You love him even though you have never seen him; though not seeing him, you trust him; and even now you are happy with the inexpressible joy that comes from heaven itself.* (1 Peter 1:8 TLB)

118. *You will go out in joy and be led forth in peace; the mountains and hills will burst into song before you, and all the trees of the field will clap their hands.*

(Isaiah 55:12 NIV)

119. *And the angel said unto them, Fear not: for, behold, I bring you good tidings of great joy, which shall be to all people.* (Luke 2:10 KJV)

120. *For the kingdom of God is not a matter of eating and drinking, but of righteousness, peace and joy in the Holy Spirit.* (Romans 14:17 NIV)

121. *And the ransomed of the LORD shall return, and come to Zion with songs and everlasting joy upon their heads: they shall obtain joy and gladness, and sorrow and sighing shall flee away.* (Isaiah 35:10 KJV)

PEACE

122. *The LORD blesses his people with peace.*
(Psalm 29:11 NIV)

123. *He will keep in perfect peace all those who trust in him, whose thoughts turn often to the Lord!* (Isaiah 26:3 TLB)

124. *He was wounded and bruised for our sins. He was beaten that we might have peace.*
(Isaiah 53:5 TLB)

125. *You will experience God's peace, which is far more wonderful than the human mind can understand. His peace will keep your thoughts and your hearts quiet and at rest as you trust in Christ Jesus.*

(Philippians 4:7 TLB)

126. *Since we have been made right in God's sight by faith in his promises, we can have real peace with him because of what Jesus Christ our Lord has done for us.*

(Romans 5:1 TLB)

127. *All who humble themselves before the Lord shall be given every blessing and shall have wonderful peace.* (Psalm 37:11 TLB)

128. *Peace I leave with you, my peace I give unto you: not as the world giveth, give I unto you. Let not your heart be troubled, neither let it be afraid.* (John 14:27 KJV)

129. *He promises peace to his people, his saints.* (Psalm 85:8 NIV)

130. *The mind controlled by the Spirit is life and peace.* (Romans 8:6 NIV)

131. *The fruit of the Spirit is...peace.* (Galatians 5:22 KJV)

HOPE

132. *Christ in your hearts is your only hope of glory.* (Colossians 1:27 TLB)

133. *We rejoice in the hope of the glory of God....And hope does not disappoint us, because God has poured out his love into our hearts by the Holy Spirit, whom he has given us.* (Romans 5:2, 5 NIV)

134. *O Lord, you alone are my hope; I've trusted you from childhood.* (Psalm 71:5 TLB)

135. *May the God of hope fill you with all joy and peace as you trust in him, so that you may overflow with hope by the power of the Holy Spirit.* (Romans 15:13 NIV)

136. *"For I know the plans I have for you," says the Lord. "They are plans for good and not for evil, to give you a future and a hope."* (Jeremiah 29:11 TLB)

137. *For everything that was written in the past was written to teach us, so that through endurance and the encouragement of the Scriptures we might have hope.* (Romans 15:4 NIV)

138. *Praise be to the God and Father of our Lord Jesus Christ! In his great mercy he has given us new birth into a living hope through the resurrection of Jesus Christ from the dead.* (1 Peter 1:3 NIV)

139. *We who have fled to take hold of the hope offered to us may be greatly encouraged. We have this hope as an anchor for the soul, firm and secure.* (Hebrews 6:18–19 NIV)

140. *And I know that after this body has decayed, this body shall see God! Then he will be on my side! Yes, I shall see him, not*

as a stranger, but as a friend! What a glorious hope! (Job 19:26–27 TLB)

141. *I pray also that the eyes of your heart may be enlightened in order that you may know the hope to which he has called you, the riches of his glorious inheritance in the saints.* (Ephesians 1:18 NIV)

God Promises Future Blessings

ETERNAL LIFE

142. *For God so loved the world, that he gave his only begotten Son, that whosoever believeth in him should not perish, but have everlasting life.* (John 3:16 KJV)

143. *This is the promise that he hath promised us, even eternal life.* (1 John 2:25 KJV)

144. *And what is it that God has said? That he has given us eternal life and that this life is in his Son. So whoever has God's Son has life; whoever does not have his Son, does not have life.* (1 John 5:11, 12 TLB)

145. *My sheep hear my voice, and I know them, and they follow me: and I give unto them eternal life; and they shall never perish.* (John 10:27–28 KJV)

146. *For the wages of sin is death; but the gift of God is eternal life through Jesus Christ our Lord.* (Romans 6:23 KJV)

147. *I tell you the truth, whoever hears my word and believes him who sent me has eternal life and will not be condemned; he has crossed over from death to life.*
(John 5:24 NIV)

148. *The man who loves his life will lose it, while the man who hates his life in this world will keep it for eternal life.*
(John 12:25 NIV)

LIFE AFTER DEATH

149. *And if the Spirit of God, who raised up Jesus from the dead, lives in you, he will make your dying bodies live again after you die, by means of this same Holy Spirit living within you.* (Romans 8:11 TLB)

150. *It will all happen in a moment, in the twinkling of an eye, when the last trumpet is blown. For there will be a trumpet blast from the sky, and all the Christians who have died will suddenly become alive, with new bodies that will never, never die; and then we who are still alive shall suddenly*

*have new bodies too. For our earthly bod-
ies, the ones we have now that can die,
must be transformed into heavenly bodies
that cannot perish but will live forever.*
(1 Corinthians 15:52–53 TLB)

151. *Jesus said to her, "I am the resurrection
and the life. He who believes in me will
live, even though he dies; and whoever
lives and believes in me will never die. Do
you believe this?"* (John 11:25–26 NIV)

152. *For since we believe that Jesus died and
then came back to life again, we can also
believe that when Jesus returns, God will
bring back with him all the Christians
who have died.* (1 Thessalonians 4:14 TLB)

153. *We know that the same God who brought
the Lord Jesus back from death will also
bring us back to life again with Jesus.*
(2 Corinthians 4:14 TLB)

JESUS' RETURN

154. *For the Lord himself will come down from
heaven, with a loud command, with the
voice of the archangel and with the trumpet
call of God....So we will be with the Lord
forever.* (1 Thessalonians 4:16–17 NIV)

155. *For as the lightning comes from the east is visible even in the west, so will be the coming of the Son of Man....At that time the sign of the Son of Man will appear in the sky, and all the nations of the earth will mourn. They will see the Son of Man coming on the clouds of the sky, with power and great glory.* (Matthew 24:27, 30 NIV)

156. *Remember what I told you—I am going away, but I will come back to you again.*
(John 14:28 TLB)

157. *In my Father's house are many mansions: if it were not so, I would have told you. I go to prepare a place for you. And if I go and prepare a place for you, I will come again, and receive you unto myself; that where I am, there ye may also be.* (John 14:2–3 KJV)

158. *This same Jesus, who has been taken from you into heaven, will come back in the same way you have seen him go into heaven.* (Acts 1:11 NIV)

159. *Look, he is coming with the clouds, and every eye will see him.* (Revelation 1:7 NIV)

160. *And when Christ who is our real life comes back again, you will shine with him and share in all his glories.* (Colossians 3:4 TLB)

161. *He will appear a second time...to bring salvation to those who are waiting for him.*
(Hebrews 9:28 NIV)

HEAVEN

162. *God has reserved for his children the priceless gift of eternal life; it is kept in heaven for you, pure and undefiled, beyond the reach of change and decay. And God, in his mighty power, will make sure that you get there safely to receive it because you are trusting him.* (1 Peter 1:4–5 TLB)

163. *So, dear brothers, work hard to prove that you really are among those God has called and chosen, and then you will never stumble or fall away. And God will open wide the gates of heaven for you to enter into the eternal kingdom of our Lord and Savior Jesus Christ.* (2 Peter 1:10–11 TLB)

164. *This world is not our home; we are looking forward to our everlasting home in heaven.*
(Hebrews 13:14 TLB)

165. *I saw the Holy City, the new Jerusalem, coming down out of heaven from God, prepared as a bride beautifully dressed for her husband. And I heard a loud voice from*

the throne saying, "Now the dwelling of God is with men, and he will live with them. They will be his people, and God himself will be with them and be their God." (Revelation 21:2–3 NIV)

166. *In keeping with his promise we are looking forward to a new heaven and a new earth, the home of righteousness.*

(2 Peter 3:13 NIV)

167. *And Jesus replied, "Today you will be with me in Paradise. This is a solemn promise."*

(Luke 23:43 TLB)

God Promises Personal Blessings

STRENGTH

168. *The LORD gives strength to his people.*
(Psalm 29:11 NIV)

169. *Trust in the Lord God always, for in the Lord Jehovah is your everlasting strength.*
(Isaiah 26:4 TLB)

170. *The LORD is my strength and my shield; my heart trusted in him, and I am helped: therefore my heart greatly rejoiceth; and with my song will I praise him.*
(Psalm 28:7 KJV)

171. *The joy of the LORD is your strength.*
(Nehemiah 8:10 KJV)

172. *Be strong in the Lord, and in the power of his might.* (Ephesians 6:10 KJV)

173. *He gives strength to the weary and increases the power of the weak.*

(Isaiah 40:29 NIV)

174. *They that wait upon the LORD shall renew their strength; they shall mount up with wings as eagles; they shall run, and not be weary; and they shall walk, and not faint.*

(Isaiah 40:31 KJV)

175. *I can do all things through Christ which strengtheneth me.*   (Philippians 4:13 KJV)

176. *My flesh and my heart may fail, but God is the strength of my heart and my portion forever.*   (Psalm 73:26 NIV)

177. *The LORD will...strengthen your frame. You will be like a well-watered garden, like a spring whose waters never fail.*

(Isaiah 58:11 NIV)

CONFIDENCE

178. *This is the confidence that we have in him, that, if we ask any thing according to his will, he heareth us: and if we know that he hear us, whatsoever we ask, we know that we have the petitions that we desired of him.*   (1 John 5:14–15 KJV)

179. *In the fear of the LORD is strong confidence: and his children shall have a place of refuge.* (Proverbs 14:26 KJV)

180. *The Lord God, the Holy One of Israel, says: "Only in returning to me and waiting for me will you be saved; in quietness and confidence is your strength."*
(Isaiah 30:15 TLB)

181. *Being confident of this, that he who began a good work in you will carry it on to completion until the day of Christ Jesus.*
(Philippians 1:6 NIV)

182. *Have no fear of sudden disaster or of the ruin that overtakes the wicked, for the LORD will be your confidence and will keep your foot from being snared.*
(Proverbs 3:25–26 NIV)

183. *Dear friends, if our hearts do not condemn us, we have confidence before God and receive from him anything we ask, because we obey his commands and do what pleases him.* (1 John 3:21–22 NIV)

WISDOM

184. *To the man who pleases him, God gives wisdom.* (Ecclesiastes 2:26 NIV)

185. *For the Lord grants wisdom! His every word is a treasure of knowledge and understanding. He grants good sense to the godly.* (Proverbs 2:6–7 TLB)

186. *For the reverence and fear of God are basic to all wisdom. Knowing God results in every other kind of understanding.*
(Proverbs 9:10 TLB)

187. *But true wisdom and power are God's. He alone knows what we should do; he understands.* (Job 12:13 TLB)

188. *Praise be to the name of God for ever and ever; wisdom and power are his....He gives wisdom to the wise and knowledge to the discerning. He reveals deep and hidden things.* (Daniel 2:20–22 NIV)

189. *He shows how to distinguish right from wrong, how to find the right decision every time. For wisdom and truth will enter the very center of your being, filling your life with joy.* (Proverbs 2:9–10 TLB)

190. *You are in Christ Jesus, who has become for us wisdom from God.*
(1 Corinthians 1:30 NIV)

191. *We know about these things because God has sent his Spirit to tell us, and his Spirit*

searches out and shows us all of God's deepest secrets.   (1 Corinthians 2:10 TLB)

192. *If any of you lacks wisdom, he should ask God, who gives generously to all without finding fault, and it will be given to him.*
(James 1:5 NIV)

193. *I will bless the Lord who counsels me; he gives me wisdom in the night. He tells me what to do.*   (Psalm 16:7 TLB)

INSTRUCTION

194. *Who, then, is the man that fears the LORD? He will instruct him in the way chosen for him.*   (Psalm 25:12 NIV)

195. *I will instruct you and teach you in the way you should go; I will counsel you and watch over you.*   (Psalm 32:8 NIV)

196. *All scripture is given by inspiration of God, and is profitable for doctrine, for re-proof, for correction, for instruction in righteousness: that the man of God may be perfect, thoroughly furnished unto all good works.*   (2 Timothy 3:16–17 KJV)

197. *The Lord Almighty is a wonderful teacher.*
(Isaiah 28:29 TLB)

198. *Good and upright is the LORD; therefore he instructs sinners in his ways. He guides the humble in what is right and teaches them his way.* (Psalm 25:8–9 NIV)

199. *He that refuseth instruction despiseth his own soul: but he that heareth reproof getteth understanding. The fear of the LORD is the instruction of wisdom; and before honour is humility.* (Proverbs 15:32–33 KJV)

200. *Listen to advice and accept instruction, and in the end you will be wise. Many are the plans in a man's heart, but it is the Lord's purpose that prevails.* (Proverbs 19:20–21 NIV)

GUIDANCE

201. *He guides the humble in what is right and teaches them his way.* (Psalm 25:9 NIV)

202. *I will...guide you along the best pathway for your life; I will advise you and watch your progress.* (Psalm 32:8 TLB)

203. *If I rise on the wings of the dawn, if I settle on the far side of the sea, even there your hand will guide me, your right hand will hold me fast.* (Psalm 139:9–10 NIV)

204. *For this great God is our God forever and ever. He will be our guide until we die.*
(Psalm 48:14 TLB)

205. *You will keep on guiding me all my life with your wisdom and counsel, and afterwards receive me into the glories of heaven!* (Psalm 73:24 TLB)

206. *The LORD is my shepherd....He guides me in paths of righteousness for his name's sake.* (Psalm 23:1, 3 NIV)

207. *Thine ears shall hear a word behind thee, saying, This is the way, walk ye in it, when ye turn to the right hand, and when ye turn to the left.* (Isaiah 30:21 KJV)

SUCCESS

208. *Do not let this Book of the Law depart from your mouth; meditate on it day and night, so that you may be careful to do everything written in it. Then you will be prosperous and successful.* (Joshua 1:8 NIV)

209. *Have faith in the LORD your God and you will be upheld; have faith in his prophets and you will be successful.*
(2 Chronicles 20:20 NIV)

210. *In everything you do, put God first, and he will direct you and crown your efforts with success.*   (Proverbs 3:6 TLB)

211. *Commit to the LORD whatever you do, and your plans will succeed.*
                          (Proverbs 16:3 NIV)

212. *Our only power and success comes from God.*   (2 Corinthians 3:5 TLB)

213. *Keep the law of the LORD your God. Then you will have success.*
                    (1 Chronicles 22:12–13 NIV)

HONOR

214. *The LORD declares: "...Those who honor me I will honor."*   (1 Samuel 2:30 NIV)

215. *Jesus replied..."Whoever serves me must follow me; and where I am, my servant also will be. My Father will honor the one who serves me."*   (John 12:23, 26 NIV)

216. *"Because he loves me," says the LORD,..."I will deliver him and honor him."*
                          (Psalm 91:14–15 NIV)

217. *All who fear God and trust in him are blessed beyond expression....His deeds will*

*never be forgotten. He shall have influence
and honor.* (Psalm 112:1, 9 TLB)

218. *Humility and reverence for the Lord will
make you both wise and honored.*
(Proverbs 15:33 TLB)

219. *Blessed is the man who finds wisdom, the
man who gains understanding....Long life
is in her right hand; in her left hand are
riches and honor.* (Proverbs 3:13, 16 NIV)

220. *He who ignores discipline comes to poverty
and shame, but whoever heeds correction
is honored.* (Proverbs 13:18 NIV)

SATISFACTION

221. *The Lord will guide you continually, and
satisfy you with all good things...and you
will be like a well-watered garden, like an
ever-flowing spring.* (Isaiah 58:11 TLB)

222. *He fills my life with good things! My youth
is renewed like the eagle's!*
(Psalm 103:5 TLB)

223. *Why spend money on what is not bread,
and your labor on what does not satisfy?
Listen, listen to me, and eat what is good,*

and your soul will delight in the richest of
fare. (Isaiah 55:2 NIV)

224. *Stay away from the love of money; be satis-
fied with what you have. For God has said,
"I will never, never fail you nor forsake
you."* (Hebrews 13:5 TLB)

225. *And Jesus said unto them, I am the bread
of life: he that cometh to me shall never
hunger; and he that believeth on me shall
never thirst.* (John 6:35 KJV)

226. *Oh, that these men would praise the Lord
for his loving-kindness, and for all of his
wonderful deeds! For he satisfies the
thirsty soul and fills the hungry soul with
good.* (Psalm 107:8–9 TLB)

COMFORT

227. *Remember your word to your servant, for
you have given me hope. My comfort in my
suffering is this: Your promise preserves
my life.* (Psalm 119:49–50 NIV)

228. *I, even I, am he who comforts you and
gives you all this joy. So what right have
you to fear mere mortal men, who wither
like the grass and disappear?*
(Isaiah 51:12 TLB)

229. *In the multitude of my thoughts within me thy comforts delight my soul.*

(Psalm 94:19 KJV)

230. *I will not leave you comfortless: I will come to you.* (John 14:18 KJV)

231. *Shout for joy, O heavens; rejoice, O earth; burst into song, O mountains! For the LORD comforts his people and will have compassion on his afflicted ones.*

(Isaiah 49:13 NIV)

232. *Praise be to the God and Father of our Lord Jesus Christ, the Father of compassion and the God of all comfort, who comforts us in all our troubles, so that we can comfort those in any trouble with the comfort we ourselves have received from God.*

(2 Corinthians 1:3–4 NIV)

233. *Blessed are they that mourn: for they shall be comforted.* (Matthew 5:4 KJV)

234. *May our Lord Jesus Christ himself and God our Father, who has loved us and given us everlasting comfort and hope, which we don't deserve, comfort your hearts with all comfort, and help you in every good thing you say and do.*

(2 Thessalonians 2:16–17 TLB)

YOUR HEART'S DESIRE

235. *Delight yourself in the LORD and he will give you the desires of your heart.*
                    (Psalm 37:4 NIV)

236. *He fulfills the desires of those who fear him; he hears their cry and saves them.*
                    (Psalm 145:19 NIV)

237. *You have granted him the desire of his heart and have not withheld the request of his lips.*   (Psalm 21:2 NIV)

238. *You open your hand and satisfy the desires of every living thing.*   (Psalm 145:16 NIV)

239. *The desire of the righteous shall be granted.*   (Proverbs 10:24 KJV)

240. *Praise the LORD...who satisfies your desires with good things so that your youth is renewed like the eagle's.*   (Psalm 103:1, 5 NIV)

241. *May the Lord be with you!...May he grant you your heart's desire and fulfill all your plans.*   (Psalm 20:1, 4 TLB)

242. *I say unto you, What things soever ye desire, when ye pray, believe that ye receive them, and ye shall have them.*
                    (Mark 11:24 KJV)

243. *And I will give you a new heart—I will give you new and right desires.*
(Ezekiel 36:26 TLB)

244. *However, as for you, I will take you, and you will rule over all that your heart desires.* (1 Kings 11:37 NIV)

245. *Since this is your heart's desire and you have not asked for wealth, riches or honor, ...therefore wisdom and knowledge will be given you. And I will also give you wealth, riches and honor.*
(2 Chronicles 1:11–12 NIV)

FAMILY BLESSINGS

246. *He* [the Lord] *blesses the home of the righteous.* (Proverbs 3:33 NIV)

247. *All your sons will be taught by the LORD, and great will be your children's peace.*
(Isaiah 54:13 NIV)

248. *Be careful to obey all these regulations I am giving you, so that it may always go well with you and your children after you, because you will be doing what is good and right in the eyes of the LORD your God.*
(Deuteronomy 12:28 NIV)

249. *Happy is the man who delights in doing [God's] commands. His children shall be honored everywhere, for good men's sons have a special heritage.*

(Psalm 112:1–2 TLB)

250. *The house of the righteous stands firm.*

(Proverbs 12:7 NIV)

251. *Our families will continue; generation after generation will be preserved by your protection.*   (Psalm 102:28 TLB)

252. *Train up a child in the way he should go: and when he is old, he will not depart from it.*   (Proverbs 22:6 KJV)

God Promises Physical Blessings

HEALTH

253. *"I will restore you to health and heal your wounds," declares the LORD.*
(Jeremiah 30:17 NIV)

254. *The Lord will...keep you healthy too; and you will be like a well-watered garden, like an ever-flowing spring.* (Isaiah 58:11 TLB)

255. *If you pay attention to these laws and are careful to follow them,...the LORD will keep you free from every disease.*
(Deuteronomy 7:12, 15 NIV)

256. *Nevertheless, I will bring health and healing to it; I will heal my people and will let them enjoy abundant peace and security.*
(Jeremiah 33:6 NIV)

257. *Then your light will break forth like the dawn, and your healing will quickly appear.* (Isaiah 58:8 NIV)

258. *Because thou hast made the LORD, which is my refuge, even the most High, thy habitation; there shall no evil befall thee, neither shall any plague come nigh thy dwelling.*
(Psalm 91:9–10 KJV)

259. *Dear friend, I pray that you may enjoy good health and that all may go well with you, even as your soul is getting along well.* (3 John 2 NIV)

HEALING

260. *I am the LORD, who heals you.*
(Exodus 15:26 NIV)

261. *He sent his word, and healed them.*
(Psalm 107:20 KJV)

262. *For you who fear my name, the Sun of Righteousness will rise with healing in his wings.* (Malachi 4:2 TLB)

263. *He himself bore our sins in his body on the tree, so that we might die to sins and live for righteousness; by his wounds you have been healed.* (1 Peter 2:24 NIV)

264. *Heal me, O LORD, and I shall be healed;*
     save me, and I shall be saved: for thou art
     my praise. (Jeremiah 17:14 KJV)

265. *Praise the LORD, O my soul, and forget not*
     all his benefits—who forgives all your sins
     and heals all your diseases.
     (Psalm 103:2–3 NIV)

266. *"I have seen his ways, but I will heal him; I*
     will guide him and restore comfort to him,
     creating praise on the lips of the mourners
     in Israel. Peace, peace, to those far and
     near," says the LORD. "And I will heal
     them." (Isaiah 57:18–19 NIV)

267. *Jesus went throughout Galilee, teaching in*
     their synagogues, preaching the good news
     of the kingdom, and healing every disease
     and sickness among the people.
     (Matthew 4:23 NIV)

268. *He was wounded for our transgressions,*
     he was bruised for our iniquities: the chas-
     tisement of our peace was upon him; and
     with his stripes we are healed.
     (Isaiah 53:5 KJV)

269. *Therefore confess your sins to each other*
     and pray for each other so that you may be
     healed. The prayer of a righteous man is
     powerful and effective. (James 5:16 NIV)

SAFETY

270. *The Lord is my fort where I can enter and be safe; no one can follow me in and slay me. He is a rugged mountain where I hide; he is my Savior, a rock where none can reach me, and a tower of safety. He is my shield.* (Psalm 18:2 TLB)

271. *I will lie down and sleep in peace, for you alone, O LORD, make me dwell in safety.* (Psalm 4:8 NIV)

272. *The LORD your God...will give you rest from all your enemies around you so that you will live in safety.* (Deuteronomy 12:10 NIV)

273. *The name of the LORD is a strong tower; the righteous run to it and are safe.* (Proverbs 18:10 NIV)

274. *Though I am surrounded by troubles, you will bring me safely through them. You will clench your fist against my angry enemies! Your power will save me.* (Psalm 138:7 TLB)

275. *We live within the shadow of the Almighty, sheltered by the God who is above all gods. This I declare, that he alone is my refuge,*

my place of safety; he is my God, and I am
trusting him.   (Psalm 91:1–2 TLB)

276. *Fear of man will prove to be a snare, but
whoever trusts in the LORD is kept safe.*
(Proverbs 29:25 NIV)

277. *If you devote your heart to him and stretch
out your hands to him,…then you will lift
up your face without shame; you will stand
firm and without fear….You will be secure,
because there is hope; you will look about
you and take your rest in safety.*
(Job 11:13, 15, 18 NIV)

PROTECTION

278. *Jehovah himself is caring for you! He is
your defender. He protects you day and
night. He keeps you from all evil, and preserves your life. He keeps his eye upon you
as you come and go and always guards
you.*   (Psalm 121:5–8 TLB)

279. *Those who trust in the Lord are steady as
Mount Zion, unmoved by any circum-
stance. Just as the mountains surround
and protect Jerusalem, so the Lord surrounds and protects his people.*
(Psalm 125:1–2 TLB)

280. [God] *rescues you from every trap and protects you from the fatal plague. He will shield you with his wings! They will shelter you. His faithful promises are your armor.* (Psalm 91:3–4 TLB)

281. *For the LORD loves the just and will not forsake his faithful ones. They will be protected forever.* (Psalm 37:28 NIV)

282. *He will protect his godly ones, but the wicked shall be silenced in darkness. No one shall succeed by strength alone.*
(1 Samuel 2:9 TLB)

283. *He orders his angels to protect you wherever you go. They will steady you with their hands to keep you from stumbling against the rocks on the trail.*
(Psalm 91:11–12 TLB)

284. *For who is God except our Lord? Who but he is as a rock? He fills me with strength and protects me wherever I go.*
(Psalm 18:31–32 TLB)

285. *Blessed is the Lord, for he has shown me that his never-failing love protects me like the walls of a fort!...Oh, love the Lord, all of you who are his people; for the Lord protects those who are loyal to him.*
(Psalm 31:21, 23 TLB)

LONG LIFE

286. *The fear of the LORD adds length to life, but the years of the wicked are cut short.*
(Proverbs 10:27 NIV)

287. *"Because he loves me," says the LORD, ..."With long life will I satisfy him and show him my salvation."*
(Psalm 91:14, 16 NIV)

288. *True humility and respect for the Lord lead a man to riches, honor, and long life.*
(Proverbs 22:4 TLB)

289. *The fear of the LORD is the beginning of wisdom, and knowledge of the Holy One is understanding. For through me your days will be many, and years will be added to your life.*
(Proverbs 9:10–11 NIV)

290. *If you exalt wisdom, she will exalt you. ...Do as I say, and you will have a long, good life.*
(Proverbs 4:8, 10 TLB)

291. *Honor your father and mother. This is the first of God's Ten Commandments that ends with a promise. And this is the promise: that if you honor your father and mother, yours will be a long life, full of blessing.*
(Ephesians 6:2–3 TLB)

CHILDREN

292. *Your wife will be like a fruitful vine within your house; your sons will be like olive shoots around your table.* (Psalm 128:3 NIV)

293. *Children are a gift from God; they are his reward. Children born to a young man are like sharp arrows to defend him. Happy is the man who has his quiver full of them.* (Psalm 127:3–5 TLB)

294. *The LORD your God will...increase your numbers. He will bless the fruit of your womb....None of your men or women will be childless.* (Deuteronomy 7:12–14 NIV)

295. *He gives children to the childless wife, so that she becomes a happy mother.* (Psalm 113:9 TLB)

296. *The LORD shall increase you more and more, you and your children.* (Psalm 115:14 KJV)

297. *You shall serve the Lord your God only.... There will be no miscarriages nor barrenness throughout your land.* (Exodus 23:25–26 TLB)

298. *He hath blessed thy children within thee.* (Psalm 147:13 KJV)

God Promises Material Blessings

ABUNDANCE

299. *My God shall supply all your need according to his riches in glory by Christ Jesus.*
                              (Philippians 4:19 KJV)

300. *Seek ye first the kingdom of God, and his righteousness; and all these things shall be added unto you.*   (Matthew 6:33 KJV)

301. *If you fully obey all of these commandments of the Lord your God,...the Lord will give you an abundance of good things in the land, just as he promised: many children, many cattle, and abundant crops. He will open to you his wonderful treasury of rain in the heavens, to give you fine crops every season. He will bless everything you do.*   (Deuteronomy 28:1, 11–12 TLB)

302. *Jehovah God is our Light and our Protector. He gives us grace and glory. No good thing will he withhold from those who walk along his paths.* (Psalm 84:11 TLB)

303. *Fear the LORD, you his saints, for those who fear him lack nothing. The lions may grow weak and hungry, but those who seek the LORD lack no good thing.*

(Psalm 34:9–10 NIV)

304. *All mankind scratches for its daily bread, but your heavenly Father knows your needs. He will always give you all you need from day to day if you will make the Kingdom of God your primary concern.*

(Luke 12:30–31 TLB)

PROSPERITY

305. *If you fully obey the LORD your God and carefully follow all his commands...the LORD your God will set you high above all the nations on earth....The LORD will grant you abundant prosperity.*

(Deuteronomy 28:1, 11 NIV)

306. *Believe in the LORD your God, so shall ye be established; believe his prophets, so shall ye prosper.* (2 Chronicles 20:20 KJV)

307. *If you pay attention to the commands of the
     LORD your God that I give you this day
     and carefully follow them, you will always
     be at the top, never at the bottom.*
     (Deuteronomy 28:13 NIV)

308. *Blessed are all who fear the LORD, who
     walk in his ways. You will eat the fruit of
     your labor; blessings and prosperity will be
     yours.* (Psalm 128:1–2 NIV)

309. *Blessed is the man that walketh not in the
     counsel of the ungodly....But his delight is
     the law of the LORD; and in his law doth
     he meditate day and night. And he shall be
     like a tree planted by the rivers of water,
     that bringeth forth his fruit in his season;
     his leaf also shall not wither; and whatso-
     ever he doeth shall prosper.*
     (Psalm 1:1–3 KJV)

310. *Carefully follow the terms of this covenant,
     so that you may prosper in everything you
     do.* (Deuteronomy 29:9 NIV)

FOOD

311. *He gives food to those who trust him; he
     never forgets his promises.*
     (Psalm 111:5 TLB)

312. *In all my years I have never seen the Lord forsake a man who loves him; nor have I seen the children of the godly go hungry.*
(Psalm 37:25 TLB)

313. *Therefore I say unto you, Take no thought for your life, what ye shall eat, or what ye shall drink....Is not the life more than meat?...Behold the fowls of the air; for they sow not, neither do they reap, nor gather into barns; yet your heavenly Father feedeth them. Are ye not much better then they?* (Matthew 6:25–26 KJV)

314. *The days of the blameless are known to the LORD, and their inheritance will endure forever. In times of disaster they will not wither; in days of famine they will enjoy plenty.* (Psalm 37:18–19 NIV)

315. *So do not worry, saying, "What shall we eat?" or "What shall we drink?"...For the pagans run after all these things, and your heavenly Father knows that you need them. But seek first his kingdom and his righteousness, and all these things will be given to you as well.* (Matthew 6:31–33 NIV)

316. *He is the God who keeps every promise, who gives justice to the poor and oppressed and food to the hungry.* (Psalm 146:6–7 TLB)

317. *If you are willing and obedient, you will eat the best from the land.* (Isaiah 1:19 NIV)

HARVEST

318. *As long as the earth remains, there will be springtime and harvest, cold and heat, winter and summer, day and night.*
(Genesis 8:22 TLB)

319. *If you obey all of my commandments, I will give you regular rains, and the land will yield bumper crops, and the trees will be loaded with fruit long after the normal time! And grapes will still be ripening when sowing time comes again.*
(Leviticus 26:3–5 TLB)

320. *Because of your obedience, the Lord your God will keep his part of the contract....He will make you fertile and give fertility to your ground and to your animals, so that you will have large crops of grain, grapes, and olives, and great flocks of cattle, sheep, and goats.* (Deuteronomy 7:12–13 TLB)

321. *He will also send you rain for the seed you sow in the ground, and the food that comes from the land will be rich and plentiful.*
(Isaiah 30:23 NIV)

322. *He makes grass grow for the cattle, and plants for man to cultivate—bringing forth food from the earth.* (Psalm 104:14 NIV)

323. *I will look on you with favor and make you fruitful and increase your numbers, and I will keep my covenant with you. You will still be eating last year's harvest when you will have to move it out to make room for the new.* (Leviticus 26:9–10 NIV)

324. *Ask the LORD for rain in the springtime; it is the LORD who makes the storm clouds. He gives showers of rain to men, and plants of the field to everyone.* (Zechariah 10:1 NIV)

God's Promises When You Feel...

AFRAID

325. *I am the LORD, your God, who takes hold of your right hand and says to you, Do not fear; I will help you.* (Isaiah 41:13 NIV)

326. *When I am afraid, I will put my confidence in you. Yes, I will trust the promises of God. And since I am trusting him, what can mere man do to me?* (Psalm 56:3–4 TLB)

327. *The LORD is my light and my salvation; whom shall I fear? the LORD is the strength of my life; of whom shall I be afraid?* (Psalm 27:1 KJV)

328. *Fear not: for I have redeemed thee, I have called thee by name; thou art mine.* (Isaiah 43:1 KJV)

329. *He will shield you with his wings! They will shelter you. His faithful promises are your armor. Now you don't need to be afraid of the dark any more, nor fear the dangers of the day; nor dread the plagues of darkness, nor disasters in the morning.*
(Psalm 91:4–6 TLB)

330. *All who...trust in [God] are blessed beyond expression....Such a man will not be overthrown by evil circumstances. God's constant care of him will make a deep impression on all who see it. He does not fear bad news, nor live in dread of what may happen. For he is settled in his mind that Jehovah will take care of him. That is why he is not afraid but can calmly face his foes.*
(Psalm 112:1, 6–8 TLB)

331. *Do not fear, for I am with you; do not be dismayed, for I am your God. I will strengthen you and help you; I will uphold you with my righteous right hand.*
(Isaiah 41:10 NIV)

332. *Are not five sparrows sold for two pennies? Yet not one of them is forgotten by God. Indeed, the very hairs of your heard are all numbered. Don't be afraid; you are worth more than many sparrows.*
(Luke 12:6–7 NIV)

333. *God hath not given us the spirit of fear;
     but of power, and of love, and of a sound
     mind.*   (2 Timothy 1:7 KJV)

334. *There is no fear in love. But perfect love
     drives out fear.*   (1 John 4:18 NIV)

BROKENHEARTED

335. *The LORD is close to the brokenhearted
     and saves those who are crushed in spirit.*
                            (Psalm 34:18 NIV)

336. *You have seen me tossing and turning
     through the night. You have collected all
     my tears and preserved them in your bot-
     tle! You have recorded every one in your
     book....This one thing I know: God is for
     me! I am trusting God—oh, praise his
     promises!*   (Psalm 56:8–10 TLB)

337. *The Spirit of the Lord is upon me; he has
     appointed me to preach Good News to the
     poor; he has sent me to heal the broken-
     hearted and to announce that captives
     shall be released and the blind shall see,
     that the downtrodden shall be freed from
     their oppressors, and that God is ready to
     give blessings to all who come to him.*
                            (Luke 4:18–19 TLB)

338. *Do not let your hearts be troubled. Trust in God; trust also in me.* (John 14:1 NIV)

339. *Shout for joy, O heavens; rejoice, O earth...For the LORD comforts his people and will have compassion on his afflicted ones.* (Isaiah 49:13 NIV)

340. *It is a broken spirit you want—remorse and penitence. A broken and a contrite heart, O God, you will not ignore.*
(Psalm 51:17 TLB)

341. *The Spirit of the Lord God is upon me, because the Lord has anointed me to bring good news to the suffering and afflicted. He has sent me to comfort the brokenhearted...to tell those who mourn that the time of God's favor to them has come.*
(Isaiah 61:1–2 TLB)

342. *Praise the LORD....He heals the brokenhearted and binds up their wounds.*
(Psalm 147:1, 3 NIV)

343. *Their contempt has broken my heart; my spirit is heavy within me....But rescue me, O God, from my poverty and pain....For Jehovah hears the cries of his needy ones and does not look the other way.*
(Psalm 69:20, 29, 33 TLB)

344. *Weeping may go on all night, but in the morning there is joy.* (Psalm 30:5 TLB)

BURDENED

345. *Give your burdens to the Lord. He will carry them. He will not permit the godly to slip or fall.* (Psalm 55:22 TLB)

346. [God] *lifts the burdens from those bent down beneath their loads.*
(Psalm 146:8 TLB)

347. *Praise be to the Lord, to God our Savior, who daily bears our burdens.*
(Psalm 68:19 NIV)

348. *You have shattered the yoke that burdens them, the bar across their shoulders, the rod of their oppressor....For to us a child is born, to us a son is given, and the government will be on his shoulders. And he will be carted Wonderful Counselor, Mighty God, Everlasting Father, Prince of Peace.*
(Isaiah 9:4, 6 NIV)

349. *It is for freedom that Christ has set us free. Stand firm, then, and do not let yourselves be burdened again by a yoke of slavery.*
(Galatians 5:1 NIV)

350. *Come to me, all you who are weary and burdened, and I will give you rest. Take my yoke upon you and learn from me, for I am gentle and humble in heart, and you will find rest for your souls. For my yoke is easy and my burden is light.*

(Matthew 11:28–30 NIV)

CONFUSED

351. *God is not the author of confusion, but of peace.* (1 Corinthians 14:33 KJV)

352. *If any of you lacks wisdom, he should ask God, who gives generously to all without finding fault, and it will be given to him.*

(James 1:5 NIV)

353. *But when you ask him, be sure that you really expect him to tell you, for a doubtful mind will be as unsettled as a wave of the sea that is driven and tossed by the wind; and every decision you then make will be uncertain, as you turn first this way, and then that. If you don't ask with faith, don't expect the Lord to give you any solid answer.* (James 1:6–8 TLB)

354. *"For my thoughts are not your thoughts, neither are your ways my ways," declares*

the LORD. *"As the heavens are higher than the earth, so are my ways higher than your ways and my thoughts than your thoughts."* (Isaiah 55:8–9 NIV)

355. *The spiritual man has insight into everything, and that bothers and baffles the man of the world, who can't understand him at all....We Christians actually do have within us a portion of the very thoughts and mind of Christ.*
(1 Corinthians 2:15–16 TLB)

356. *The Lord is good and glad to teach the proper path to all who go astray; he will teach the ways that are right and best to those who humbly turn to him.*
(Psalm 25:8–9 TLB)

DEPRESSED

357. *O my soul, why be so gloomy and discouraged? Trust in God! I shall again praise him for his wondrous help; he will make me smile again, for he is my God!*
(Psalm 43:5 TLB)

358. *My health fails; my spirits droop, yet God remains! He is the strength of my heart; he is mine forever!* (Psalm 73:26 TLB)

359. *All who are oppressed may come to him. He is a refuge for them in their times of trouble. All those who know your mercy, Lord, will count on you for help. For you have never yet forsaken those who trust in you.* (Psalm 9:9–10 TLB)

360. *O my soul, don't be discouraged. Don't be upset. Expect God to act! For I know that I shall again have plenty of reason to praise him for all that he will do. He is my help! He is my God!* (Psalm 42:11 TLB)

361. *To all who mourn in Israel he will give: beauty for ashes; joy instead of mourning; praise instead of heaviness.*

(Isaiah 61:3 TLB)

362. *The joy of the Lord is your strength. You must not be dejected and sad!...That's right! Don't weep! For this is a day of holy joy, not of sadness.*

(Nehemiah 8:10–11 TLB)

363. *Be of good courage, and he shall strengthen your heart, all ye that hope in the LORD.* (Psalm 31:24 KJV)

364. *He lifted me out of the pit of despair, out from the bog and the mire, and set my feet on a hard, firm path, and steadied me as I walked along.* (Psalm 40:2 TLB)

365. *I weep with grief; my heart is heavy with sorrow; encourage and cheer me with your words.* (Psalm 119:28 TLB)

DISAPPOINTED

366. *Hope does not disappoint us, because God has poured out his love into our hearts by the Holy Spirit, whom he has given us.*
(Romans 5:5 NIV)

367. *And we know that all that happens to us is working for our good if we love God and are fitting into his plans.* (Romans 8:28 TLB)

368. *O my people, trust him all the time. Pour out your longings before him, for he can help!* (Psalm 62:8 TLB)

369. *We wait in hope for the LORD; he is our help and our shield. In him our hearts rejoice, for we trust in his holy name. May your unfailing love rest upon us, O LORD, even as we put our hope in you.*
(Psalm 33:20–22 NIV)

370. *He listened! He heard my prayer! He paid attention to it! Blessed be God, who didn't turn away when I was praying, and didn't refuse me his kindness and love.*
(Psalm 66:19–20 TLB)

371. *Without counsel purposes are disappointed: but in the multitude of counsellors they are established.*   (Proverbs 15:22 KJV)

FORSAKEN

372. *Do not be afraid or discouraged, for the LORD God, my God, is with you. He will not fail you or forsake you.*

(1 Chronicles 28:20 NIV)

373. *Those who know your name will trust in you, for you, LORD, have never forsaken those who seek you.*   (Psalm 9:10 NIV)

374. *There are "friends" who pretend to be friends, but there is a friend who sticks closer than a brother.*   (Proverbs 18:24 TLB)

375. *Be strong and courageous. Do not be afraid or terrified because of them, for the LORD your God goes with you; he will never leave you nor forsake you....The LORD himself goes before you and will be with you; he will never leave you nor forsake you. Do not be afraid; do not be discouraged.*

(Deuteronomy 31:6, 8 NIV)

376. *In all my years I have never seen the Lord forsake a man who loves him.*

(Psalm 37:25 TLB)

377. *For the LORD loves the just and will not forsake his faithful ones. They will be protected forever.* (Psalm 37:28 NIV)

378. *The Lord will work out his plans for my life—for your loving-kindness, Lord, continues forever. Don't abandon me—for you made me.* (Psalm 138:8 TLB)

379. *Can a mother forget the baby at her breast and have no compassion on the child she has borne? Though she may forget, I will not forget you! See, I have engraved you on the palms of my hands.*

(Isaiah 49:15–16 NIV)

380. *He hath said, I will never leave thee, nor forsake thee.* (Hebrews 13:5 KJV)

GUILTY

381. *Brothers! Listen! In this man Jesus, there is forgiveness for your sins! Everyone who trusts in him is freed from all guilt and declared righteous.* (Acts 13:38–39 TLB)

382. *What happiness for those whose guilt has been forgiven! What joys when sins are covered over! What relief for those who have confessed their sins and God has cleared their record.* (Psalm 32:1–2 TLB)

383. *Yes, all have sinned; all fall short of God's
glorious ideal; yet now God declares us
"not guilty" of offending him if we trust in
Jesus Christ, who in his kindness freely
takes away our sins.* (Romans 3:23–24 TLB)

384. *So there is now no condemnation awaiting
those who belong to Christ Jesus. For the
power of the life-giving Spirit—and this
power is mine through Christ Jesus—has
freed me from the vicious circle of sin and
death.* (Romans 8:1–2 TLB)

385. *Having chosen us, he called us to come to
him; and when we came, he declared us
"not guilty," filled us with Christ's goodness, gave us right standing with himself,
and promised us his glory.*
(Romans 8:30 TLB)

386. *The blood of Christ will transform our
lives and hearts. His sacrifice frees us from
the worry of having to obey the old rules
and makes us want to serve the living God.*
(Hebrews 9:14 TLB)

HELPLESS

387. *O Lord...you are known as the helper of
the helpless.* (Psalm 10:14 TLB)

388. *I am the LORD, your God, who takes hold of your right hand and says to you, Do not fear; I will help you.* (Isaiah 41:13 NIV)

389. *All who are oppressed may come to him. He is a refuge for them in their times of trouble. All those who know your mercy, Lord, will count on you for help. For you have never yet forsaken those who trust in you.* (Psalm 9:9–10 TLB)

390. *Surely God is my help; the Lord is the one who sustains me.* (Psalm 54:4 NIV)

391. *He said to me, "My grace is sufficient for you, for my power is made perfect in weakness." Therefore I will boast all the more gladly about my weaknesses, so that Christ's power may rest on me....When I am weak, then I am strong.* (2 Corinthians 12:9–10 NIV)

392. *Greater is he that is in you, than he that is in the world.* (1 John 4:4 KJV)

393. *The Holy Spirit helps us with our daily problems and in our praying. For we don't even know what we should pray for nor how to pray as we should, but the Holy Spirit prays for us with such feeling that it cannot be expressed in words.* (Romans 8:26 TLB)

394. *So let us come boldly to the very throne of God and stay there to receive his mercy and to find grace to help us in our times of need.* (Hebrews 4:16 TLB)

395. *I can do everything God asks me to with the help of Christ who gives me the strength and power.* (Philippians 4:13 TLB)

396. *So we say with confidence, "The Lord is my helper; I will not be afraid. What can man do to me?"* (Hebrews 13:6 NIV)

IMPATIENT

397. *Don't be impatient. Wait for the Lord, and he will come and save you! Be brave, stouthearted, and courageous. Yes, wait and he will help you.* (Psalm 27:14 TLB)

398. *Patience develops strength of character in us and helps us trust God more each time we use it until finally our hope and faith are strong and steady.* (Romans 5:4 TLB)

399. *Do not let this happy trust in the Lord die away, no matter what happens. Remember your reward! You need to keep on patiently doing God's will if you want him to do for you all that he has promised.*
(Hebrews 10:35–36 TLB)

400. *Don't be impatient for the Lord to act! Keep traveling steadily along his pathway and in due season he will honor you with every blessing.*   (Psalm 37:34 TLB)

401. *Rest in the LORD, and wait patiently for him.*   (Psalm 37:7 KJV)

402. *When the way is rough, your patience has a chance to grow. So let it grow, and don't try to squirm out of your problems. For when your patience is finally in full bloom, then you will be ready for anything, strong in character, full and complete.*

(James 1:3–4 TLB)

LONELY

403. *And be sure of this—that I am with you always, even to the end of the world.*

(Matthew 28:20 TLB)

404. *I, the LORD, have called you in righteousness; I will take hold of your hand. I will keep you.*   (Isaiah 42:6 NIV)

405. *"For the mountains may depart and the hills disappear, but my kindness shall not leave you. My promise of peace for you will never be broken," says the Lord who has mercy upon you.*   (Isaiah 54:10 TLB)

406. *The LORD hath appeared of old unto me, saying, Yea, I have loved thee with an everlasting love: therefore with lovingkindness have I drawn thee.* (Jeremiah 31:3 KJV)

407. *I will not abandon you or leave you as orphans in the storm—I will come to you. In just a little while I will be gone from the world, but I will still be present with you.* (John 14:18–19 TLB)

408. *God has said, "Never will I leave you."* (Hebrews 13:5 NIV)

409. *I have set the LORD always before me. Because he is at my right hand, I will not be shaken.* (Psalm 16:8 NIV)

410. *Turn to me and be gracious to me, for I am lonely and afflicted.* (Psalm 25:16 NIV)

411. *And the Lord God said, "It isn't good for man to be alone; I will make a companion for him, a helper suited to his needs."* (Genesis 2:18 TLB)

412. *When my father and mother forsake me, then the LORD will take me up.* (Psalm 27:10 KJV)

413. *God sets the lonely in families.* (Psalm 68:6 NIV)

414. *When you pass through the waters, I will be with you.* (Isaiah 43:2 NIV)

WORRIED

415. *Don't worry about anything; instead, pray about everything; tell God your needs, and don't forget to thank him for his answers. If you do this, you will experience God's peace, which is far more wonderful than the human mind can understand. His peace will keep your thoughts and your hearts quiet and at rest as you trust in Christ Jesus.* (Philippians 4:6–7 TLB)

416. *So don't be anxious about tomorrow. God will take care of your tomorrow too. Live one day at a time.* (Matthew 6:34 TLB)

417. *If you will humble yourselves under the mighty hand of God, in his good time he will lift you up. Let him have all your worries and cares, for he is always thinking about you and watching everything that concerns you.* (1 Peter 5:6–7 TLB)

418. *Don't worry at all about having enough food and clothing....Your heavenly Father already knows perfectly well that you need them, and he will give them to you if you*

give him first place in your life and live as
he wants you to.   (Matthew 6:31–33 TLB)

419. *And besides, what's the use of worrying?
What good does it do? Will it add a single
day to your life? Of course not! And if
worry can't even do such little things as
that, what's the use of worrying over big-
ger things?*   (Luke 12:25–26 TLB)

420. *In all you do, I want you to be free from
worry.*   (1 Corinthians 7:32 TLB)

God's Promises in Times of...

DOUBT

421. *Lord, when doubts fill my mind, when my heart is in turmoil, quiet me and give me renewed hope and cheer.* (Psalm 94:19 TLB)

422. *"Have faith in God," Jesus answered. "I tell you the truth, if anyone says to this mountain, 'Go, throw yourself into the sea,' and does not doubt in his heart but believes that what he says will happen, it will be done for him."* (Mark 11:22–23 NIV)

423. *Everything is possible for him who believes.* (Mark 9:23 NIV)

424. *Yes, be bold and strong! Banish fear and doubt! For remember, the Lord your God is with you wherever you go.* (Joshua 1:9 TLB)

425. *If you believe, you will receive whatever you ask for in prayer.* (Matthew 21:22 NIV)

426. *What is faith? It is the confident assurance that something we want is going to happen. It is the certainty that what we hope for is waiting for us, even though we cannot see it up ahead.* (Hebrews 11:1 TLB)

427. *Dearly loved friends, if our consciences are clear, we can come to the Lord with perfect assurance and trust, and get whatever we ask for because we are obeying him and doing the things that please him.*
(1 John 3:21–22 TLB)

TROUBLE

428. *God is our refuge and strength, a very present help in trouble.* (Psalm 46:1 KJV)

429. *The Lord saves the godly! He is their salvation and their refuge when trouble comes. Because they trust in him, he helps them and delivers them from the plots of evil men.* (Psalm 37:39–40 TLB)

430. *A righteous man may have many troubles, but the LORD delivers him from them all.*
(Psalm 34:19 NIV)

431. *I have told you these things, so that in me you may have peace. In this world you will have trouble. But take heart! I have overcome the world.* (John 16:33 NIV)

432. *"Because he loves me," says the LORD, "I will rescue him; I will protect him, for he acknowledges my name. He will call upon me, and I will answer him; I will be with him in trouble, I will deliver him and honor him."* (Psalm 91:14–15 NIV)

433. *When you go through deep waters and great trouble, I will be with you. When you go through rivers of difficulty, you will not drown! When you walk through the fire of oppression, you will not be burned up—the flames will not consume you. For I am the Lord your God, your Savior, the Holy One of Israel.* (Isaiah 43:2–3 TLB)

TEMPTATION

434. *[Jesus] understands our weaknesses since he had the same temptations we do, though he never once gave way to them and sinned. So let us come boldly to the very throne of God and stay there to receive his mercy and to find grace to help us in our times of need.* (Hebrews 4:15–16 TLB)

435. *Remember this—the wrong desires that come into your life aren't anything new and different. Many others have faced exactly the same problems before you. And no temptation is irresistible. You can trust God to keep the temptation from becoming so strong that you can't stand up against it, for he has promised this and will do what he says. He will show you how to escape temptation's power so that you can bear up patiently against it.*

(1 Corinthians 10:13 TLB)

436. *The Lord rescued Lot out of Sodom because he was a good man, sick of the terrible wickedness he saw everywhere around him day after day. So also the Lord can rescue you and me from the temptations that surround us...until the day of final judgment comes.* (2 Peter 2:7–9 TLB)

437. *Keep away from every kind of evil. May the God of peace himself make you entirely pure and devoted to God; and may your spirit and soul and body be kept strong and blameless until that day when our Lord Jesus Christ comes back again. God, who called you to become his child, will do all this for you, just as he promised.*

(1 Thessalonians 5:22–24 TLB)

438. *Happy is the man who doesn't give in and do wrong when he is tempted, for afterwards he will get as his reward the crown of life that God has promised those who love him.* (James 1:12 TLB)

SATANIC ATTACK

439. *So use every piece of God's armor to resist the enemy whenever he attacks, and when it is all over, you will still be standing up.* (Ephesians 6:13 TLB)

440. *Submit yourselves therefore to God. Resist the devil, and he will flee from you.* (James 4:7 KJV)

441. *No one who has become part of God's family makes a practice of sinning, for Christ, God's Son, holds him securely, and the devil cannot get his hands on him.* (1 John 5:18 TLB)

442. *The Lord Jesus Christ...died for our sins just as God our Father planned, and rescued us from this evil world in which we live.* (Galatians 1:3–4 TLB)

443. *The God of peace will soon crush Satan under your feet. The grace of our Lord Jesus be with you.* (Romans 16:20 NIV)

444. *I'm not asking you to take them out of the world, but to keep them safe from Satan's power. They are not part of this world any more than I am.* (John 17:15–16 TLB)

445. *We know that we are children of God and that all the rest of the world around us is under Satan's power and control.*

(1 John 5:19 TLB)

TRIAL

446. *Blessed is the man who perseveres under trial, because when he has stood the test, he will receive the crown of life that God has promised to those who love him.*

(James 1:12 NIV)

447. *We can rejoice, too, when we run into problems and trials, for we know that they are good for us—they help us learn to be patient.* (Romans 5:3 TLB)

448. *Consider it pure joy, my brothers, whenever you face trials of many kinds, because you know that the testing of your faith develops perseverance. Perseverance must finish its work so that you may be mature and complete, not lacking anything.*

(James 1:2–4 NIV)

449. [You] *are shielded by God's power until the coming of the salvation that is ready to be revealed in the last time. In this you greatly rejoice, though now for a little while you may have had to suffer grief in all kinds of trials. These have come so that your faith—of greater worth than gold, which perishes even though refined by fire—may be proved genuine and may result in praise, glory and honor when Jesus Christ is revealed.* (1 Peter 1:5–7 NIV)

SICKNESS

450. *God blesses those who are kind to the poor....He nurses them when they are sick and soothes their pains and worries.*
(Psalm 41:1, 3 TLB)

451. *And the Lord will take away all your sickness and will not let you suffer any of the diseases of Egypt.* (Deuteronomy 7:15 TLB)

452. *I will take sickness away from the midst of thee.* (Exodus 23:25 KJV)

453. *These signs will accompany those who believe...they will place their hands on sick people, and they will get well.*
(Mark 16:17–18 NIV)

454. *Is any one of you sick? He should call the elders of the church to pray over him and anoint him with oil in the name of the Lord. And the prayer offered in faith will make the sick person well; the Lord will raise him up.* (James 5:14–15 NIV)

455. *All who touched him were healed.*
(Matthew 14:36 NIV)

456. *All the sick were healed. This fulfilled the prophecy of Isaiah, "He took our sicknesses and bore our diseases."*
(Matthew 8:16–17 TLB)

DEATH

457. *It is appointed unto men once to die.*
(Hebrews 9:27 KJV)

458. *Yea, though I walk through the valley of the shadow of death, I will fear no evil: for thou art with me; thy rod and thy staff they comfort me.* (Psalm 23:4 KJV)

459. *"Where, O death, is your victory? Where, O death, is your sting?" The sting of death is sin, and the power of sin is the law. But thanks be to God! He gives us the victory through our Lord Jesus Christ.*
(1 Corinthians 15:55–57 NIV)

460. *Our earthly bodies, the ones we have now that can die, must be transformed into heavenly bodies that cannot perish but will live forever. When this happens, then at last this Scripture will come true—"Death is swallowed up in victory."*

(1 Corinthians 15:53–54 TLB)

461. *We are not afraid but are quite content to die, for then we will be at home with the Lord. So our aim is to please him always in everything we do, whether we are here in this body or away from this body and with him in heaven.*

(2 Corinthians 5:8–9 TLB)

462. *In my Father's house are many mansions: if it were not so, I would have told you. I go to prepare a place for you. And if I go and prepare a place for you, I will come again, and receive you unto myself; that where I am, there ye may be also.* (John 14:2–3 KJV)

463. *I am convinced that nothing can ever separate us from his love. Death can't, and life can't. The angels won't, and all the powers of hell itself cannot keep God's love away. ...Nothing will ever be able to separate us from the love of God demonstrated by our Lord Jesus Christ when he died for us.*

(Romans 8:38–39 TLB)

SORROW

464. *Blessed are they that mourn: for they shall be comforted.* (Matthew 5:4 KJV)

465. *You have sorrow now, but I will see you again and then you will rejoice; and no one can rob you of that joy.* (John 16:22 TLB)

466. *Those who sow in tears will reap with songs of joy. He who goes out weeping, carrying seed to sow, will return with songs of joy, carrying sheaves with him.*

    (Psalm 126:5–6 NIV)

467. *The Lord has comforted his people, and will have compassion upon them in their sorrow.* (Isaiah 49:13 TLB)

468. *The time will come when God's redeemed will all come home again. They shall come with singing to Jerusalem, filled with joy and everlasting gladness; sorrow and mourning will all disappear.*

    (Isaiah 51:11 TLB)

469. *Then maidens will dance and be glad, young men and old as well. I will turn their mourning into gladness; I will give them comfort and joy instead of sorrow.*

    (Jeremiah 31:13 NIV)

470. *Weeping may endure for a night, but joy cometh in the morning.* (Psalm 30:5 KJV)

471. *And God shall wipe away all tears from their eyes; and there shall be no more death, neither sorrow, nor crying, neither shall there be any more pain: for the former things are passed away.*

(Revelation 21:4 KJV)

BACKSLIDING

472. *I hear a voice high upon the windswept mountains, crying, crying. It is the sons of Israel who have turned their backs on God and wandered far away. "O my rebellious children, come back to me again and I will heal you from your sins."*

(Jeremiah 3:21–22 TLB)

473. *"Come, let's talk this over!" says the Lord; "no matter how deep the stain of your sins, I can take it out and make you as clean as freshly fallen snow. Even if you are stained as red as crimson, I can make you white as wool!"* (Isaiah 1:18 TLB)

474. *If you leave God's paths and go astray, you will hear a Voice behind you say, "No, this is the way; walk here."* (Isaiah 30:21 TLB)

475. *I have swept away your offenses like a cloud, your sins like the morning mist. Return to me, for I have redeemed you.*
(Isaiah 44:22 NIV)

476. *We all, like sheep, have gone astray, each of us has turned to his own way; and the LORD has laid on him the iniquity of us all.*
(Isaiah 53:6 NIV)

477. *"I have seen his ways, but I will heal him; I will guide him and restore comfort to him....Peace, peace, to those far and near,"* says the LORD. *"And I will heal them."*
(Isaiah 57:18–19 NIV)

478. *My dear children, I write this to you so that you will not sin. But if anybody does sin, we have one who speaks to the Father in our defense—Jesus Christ, the Righteous One.* (1 John 2:1 NIV)

PERSONAL ATTACK

479. *If God be for us, who can be against us?*
(Romans 8:31 KJV)

480. *The Lord saves the godly!...Because they trust in him, he helps them and delivers them from the plots of evil men.*
(Psalm 37:39–40 TLB)

481. *The LORD is my light and my salvation—whom shall I fear? The LORD is the stronghold of my life—of whom shall I be afraid? When evil men advance against me to devour my flesh, when my enemies and my foes attack me, they will stumble and fall.* (Psalm 27:1–2 NIV)

482. *Make everyone rejoice who puts his trust in you. Keep them shouting for joy because you are defending them.* (Psalm 5:11 TLB)

483. *Don't repay evil for evil. Don't snap back at those who say unkind things about you. Instead, pray for God's help for them, for we are to be kind to others, and God will bless us for it.* (1 Peter 3:9 TLB)

484. *"They will fight against you but will not overcome you, for I am with you to rescue and save you," declares the Lord. "I will save you from the hands of the wicked and redeem you from the grasp of the cruel."* (Jeremiah 15:20–21 NIV)

485. *Don't be afraid. Just stand where you are and watch, and you will see the wonderful way the Lord will rescue you today....You will never see [your enemies] again. The Lord will fight for you, and you won't need to lift a finger!* (Exodus 14:13–14 TLB)

PERSECUTION

486. *Blessed are they which are persecuted for righteousness' sake: for theirs is the kingdom of heaven.* (Matthew 5:10 KJV)

487. *Blessed are you when people insult you, persecute you and falsely say all kinds of evil against you because of me. Rejoice and be glad, because great is your reward in heaven, for in the same way they persecuted the prophets who were before you.*
(Matthew 5:11–12 NIV)

488. *Love your enemies and pray for those who persecute you, that you may be sons of your Father in heaven.* (Matthew 5:44–45 NIV)

489. *They will lay hands on you and persecute you....But make up your mind not to worry beforehand how you will defend yourselves. For I will give you words and wisdom that none of your adversaries will be able to resist or contradict.*
(Luke 21:12, 14–15 NIV)

490. *Everyone will hate you because you are mine and are called by my name. But not a hair of your head will perish! For if you stand firm, you will win your souls.*
(Luke 21:17–19 TLB)

491. *Do not be afraid of what you are about to suffer. I tell you, the devil will put some of you in prison to test you, and you will suffer persecution....Be faithful, even to the point of death, and I will give you the crown of life.* (Revelation 2:10 NIV)

492. *I am comforted by this truth, that when we suffer and die for Christ it only means that we will begin living with him in heaven. And if we think that our present service for him is hard, just remember that some day we are going to sit with him and rule with him.* (2 Timothy 2:11–12 TLB)

493. *We are pressed on every side by troubles, but not crushed and broken. We are perplexed because we don't know why things happen as they do, but we don't give up and quit. We are hunted down, but God never abandons us. We get knocked down, but we get up again and keep going.* (2 Corinthians 4:8–9 TLB)

494. *Even when we are too weak to have any faith left, he remains faithful to us and will help us, for he cannot disown us who are part of himself, and he will always carry out his promises to us.* (2 Timothy 2:13 TLB)

God's Promises for Those Who...

OBEY THE LORD

495. *When we obey him, every path he guides us on is fragrant with his loving-kindness and his truth.*   (Psalm 25:10 TLB)

496. *You are my friends if you obey me.*
                                    (John 15:14 TLB)

497. *Then he added, "Anyone who obeys my Father in heaven is my brother, sister, and mother!"*   (Matthew 12:50 TLB)

498. *The world and its desires pass away, but the man who does the will of God lives forever.*   (1 John 2:17 NIV)

499. *Those who teach God's laws and obey them shall be great in the Kingdom of Heaven.*
                                    (Matthew 5:19 TLB)

500. *Blessed are they that hear the word of God, and keep it.* (Luke 11:28 KJV)

501. *Whoever has my commands and obeys them, he is the one who loves me. He who loves me will be loved by my Father, and I too will love him and show myself to him.* (John 14:21 NIV)

502. *We know that we have come to know him if we obey his commands....But if anyone obeys his word, God's love is truly made complete in him.* (1 John 2:3, 5 NIV)

503. *If you stay in me and obey my commands, you may ask any request you like, and it will be granted!* (John 15:7 TLB)

TRUST THE LORD

504. *Many blessings are given to those who trust the Lord and have no confidence in those who are proud or who trust in idols.* (Psalm 40:4 TLB)

505. *Trust in the LORD with all your heart and lean not on your own understanding; in all your ways acknowledge him, and he will make your paths straight.* (Proverbs 3:5–6 NIV)

506. *For the Lord says, "Because he loves me, I will rescue him; I will make him great because he trusts in my name. When he calls on me I will answer; I will be with him in trouble and rescue him and honor him. I will satisfy him with a full life and give him my salvation."* (Psalm 91:14–16 TLB)

507. *Commit your way to the LORD; trust in him and he will do this: He will make your righteousness shine like the dawn, the justice of your cause like the noonday sun.*
(Psalm 37:5–6 NIV)

508. *Abiding love surrounds those who trust in the Lord.* (Psalm 32:10 TLB)

509. *Those who know your name will trust in you, for you, LORD, have never forsaken those who seek you.* (Psalm 9:10 NIV)

510. *In you our fathers put their trust; they trusted and you delivered them. They cried to you and were saved; in you they trusted and were not disappointed.*
(Psalm 22:4–5 NIV)

511. *No wonder we are happy in the Lord! For we are trusting him. We trust his holy name. Yes, Lord, let your constant love surround us, for our hopes are in you alone.* (Psalm 33:21–22 TLB)

SEEK THE LORD

512. *All who seek for God shall live in joy.*
                              (Psalm 69:32 TLB)

513. *If from there you seek the LORD your God, you will find him if you look for him with all your heart and with all your soul.*
                              (Deuteronomy 4:29 NIV)

514. *"You will seek me and find me when you seek me with all your heart. I will be found by you," declares the LORD.*
                              (Jeremiah 29:13–14 NIV)

515. *Anyone who comes to him must believe that he exists and that he rewards those who earnestly seek him.*
                              (Hebrews 11:6 NIV)

516. *I sought the LORD, and he heard me, and delivered me from all my fears....They that seek the LORD shall not want any good thing.* (Psalm 34:4, 10 KJV)

517. *But seek ye first the kingdom of God, and his righteousness; and all these things shall be added unto you.*
                              (Matthew 6:33 KJV)

518. *Let all those that seek thee rejoice and be glad in thee.* (Psalm 70:4 KJV)

519. *I love them that love me; and those that seek me early shall find me.*

(Proverbs 8:17 KJV)

WAIT ON THE LORD

520. *The Lord is wonderfully good to those who wait for him, to those who seek for him. It is good both to hope and wait quietly for the salvation of the Lord.*

(Lamentations 3:25–26 TLB)

521. *For since the beginning of the world men have not heard, nor perceived by the ear, neither hath the eye seen, O God, beside thee, what he hath prepared for him that waiteth for him.* (Isaiah 64:4 KJV)

522. *They that wait upon the LORD shall renew their strength; they shall mount up with wings as eagles; they shall run, and not be weary; and they shall walk, and not faint.*

(Isaiah 40:31 KJV)

523. *The Lord still waits for you to come to him so he can show you his love; he will conquer you to bless you, just as he said. For the Lord is faithful to his promises. Blessed are all those who wait for him to help them.* (Isaiah 30:18 TLB)

524. *My soul, wait thou only upon God; for my expectation is from him. He only is my rock and my salvation: he is my defence; I shall not be moved.* (Psalm 62:5–6 KJV)

LOVE THE LORD

525. *The LORD watches over all who love him, but all the wicked he will destroy.*
(Psalm 145:20 NIV)

526. *The Lord your God is the faithful God who for a thousand generations keeps his promises and constantly loves those who love him and who obey his commands.*
(Deuteronomy 7:9 TLB)

527. *Jesus replied, "If anyone loves me, he will obey my teaching. My Father will love him, and we will come to him and make our home with him."* (John 14:23 NIV)

528. *The man who loves God is known by God.*
(1 Corinthians 8:3 NIV)

529. *Blessed is the man who perseveres under trial, because when he has stood the test, he will receive the crown of life that God has promised to those who love him.*
(James 1:12 NIV)

111

530. *We know that in all things God works for the good of those who love him, who have been called according to his purpose.*

(Romans 8:28 NIV)

531. *It is written, Eye hath not seen, nor ear heard, neither have entered into the heart of man, the things which God hath prepared for them that love him.*

(1 Corinthians 2:9 KJV)

BELIEVE IN THE LORD

532. *If you believe that Jesus is the Christ—that he is God's Son and your Savior—then you are a child of God.* (1 John 5:1 TLB)

533. *I tell you the truth, whoever hears my word and believes him who sent me has eternal life and will not be condemned; he has crossed over from death to life.*

(John 5:24 NIV)

534. *Whoever lives and believes in me will never die.* (John 11:26 NIV)

535. *Everything is possible for him who believes.* (Mark 9:23 NIV)

536. *Those who believe in him will never be disappointed.* (Romans 9:33 TLB)

537. *Whoever believes in me, as the Scripture has said, streams of living water will flow from within him.* (John 7:38 NIV)

538. *Only we who believe God can enter into his place of rest.* (Hebrews 4:3 TLB)

539. *In solemn truth I tell you, anyone believing in me shall do the same miracles I have done, and even greater ones, because I am going to be with the Father.*

(John 14:12 TLB)

540. *Who is he that overcometh the world, but he that believeth that Jesus is the Son of God?* (1 John 5:5 KJV)

FEAR THE LORD

541. *All who fear God and trust in him are blessed beyond expression. Yes, happy is the man who delights in doing his commands.* (Psalm 112:1 TLB)

542. *The eyes of the Lord are watching over those who fear him, who rely upon his steady love.* (Psalm 33:18 TLB)

543. *The angel of the LORD encamps around those who fear him, and he delivers them.*

(Psalm 34:7 NIV)

544. *Fear the LORD, you his saints, for those who fear him lack nothing.* (Psalm 34:9 NIV)

545. *How great is your goodness, which you have stored up for those who fear you, which you bestow in the sight of men on those who take refuge in you.* (Psalm 31:19 NIV)

546. *Where is the man who fears the Lord? God will teach him how to choose the best. He shall live within God's circle of blessing, and his children shall inherit the earth.*
(Psalm 25:12–13 TLB)

547. *Blessed is every one that feareth the LORD; that walketh in his ways....It shall be well with thee.* (Psalm 128:1–2 KJV)

548. *For as the heaven is high above the earth, so great is his mercy toward them that fear him.* (Psalm 103:11 KJV)

549. *As a father has compassion on his children, so the LORD has compassion on those who fear him.* (Psalm 103:13 NIV)

PRAY TO THE LORD

550. *The earnest prayer of a righteous man has great power and wonderful results.*
(James 5:16 TLB)

551. *If my people, who are called by my name, will humble themselves and pray and seek my face and turn from their wicked ways, then will I hear from heaven and will forgive their sin and will heal their land.*

     (2 Chronicles 7:14 NIV)

552. *The Lord...delights in the prayers of his people.* (Proverbs 15:8 TLB)

553. *When you pray, go into your room, close the door and pray to your Father, who is unseen. Then your Father, who sees what is done in secret, will reward you.*

     (Matthew 6:6 NIV)

554. *If you remain in me and my words remain in you, ask whatever you wish, and it will be given you. This is to my Father's glory, that you bear much fruit, showing yourselves to be my disciples.* (John 15:7–8 NIV)

555. *Don't worry about anything; instead, pray about everything; tell God your needs, and don't forget to thank him for his answers. If you do this, you will experience God's peace, which is far more wonderful than the human mind can understand. His peace will keep your thoughts and your hearts quiet and at rest as you trust in Christ Jesus.* (Philippians 4:6–7 TLB)

556. *Build up your lives ever more strongly
     upon the foundation of our holy faith,
     learning to pray in the power and strength
     of the Holy Spirit.* (Jude 20 TLB)

SERVE THE LORD

557. *If they obey and serve him, they will spend
     the rest of their days in prosperity and their
     years in contentment.* (Job 36:11 NIV)

558. *If any man serve me, let him follow me;
     and where I am, there shall my servant be:
     if any man serve me, him will my Father
     honour.* (John 12:26 KJV)

559. *Always give yourselves fully to the work of
     the Lord, because you know that your labor
     in the Lord is not in vain.*
     (1 Corinthians 15:58 NIV)

560. *The throne of God and of the Lamb will be
     in the city, and his servants will serve him.
     They will see his face, and his name will
     be on their foreheads.*
     (Revelation 22:3–4 NIV)

561. *As for those who serve the Lord, he will
     redeem them; everyone who takes refuge in
     him will be freely pardoned.*
     (Psalm 34:22 TLB)

562. *Whatever you do, work at it with all your heart, as working for the Lord, not for men, since you know that you will receive an inheritance from the Lord as a reward. It is the Lord Christ you are serving.*

 (Colossians 3:23–24 NIV)

Do Good Deeds

563. *God blesses those who are kind to the poor. He helps them out of their troubles.*

 (Psalm 41:1 TLB)

564. *I want you to share your food with the hungry and bring right into your own homes those who are helpless, poor, and destitute. Clothe those who are cold, and don't hide from relatives who need your help. If you do these things, God will shed his own glorious light upon you. He will heal you; your godliness will lead you forward, goodness will be a shield before you, and the glory of the Lord will protect you from behind.* (Isaiah 58:7–8 TLB)

565. *Command those who are rich in this present world...to do good, to be rich in good deeds, and to be generous and willing to share. In this way they will lay up treasure for themselves as a firm foundation for the*

coming age, so that they may take hold of the life that is truly life.

(1 Timothy 6:17–19 NIV)

566. *When you help the poor you are lending to the Lord—and he pays wonderful interest on your loan!* (Proverbs 19:17 TLB)

567. *If, as my representatives, you give even a cup of cold water to a little child, you will surely be rewarded.* (Matthew 10:42 TLB)

568. *Let us not become weary in doing good, for at the proper time we will reap a harvest if we do not give up.* (Galatians 6:9 NIV)

569. *Let your light so shine before men, that they may see your good works, and glorify your Father which is in heaven.*

(Matthew 5:16 KJV)

GIVE TO OTHERS

570. *Remember the words of the Lord Jesus, how he said, It is more blessed to give than to receive.* (Acts 20:35 KJV)

571. *Whoever sows sparingly will also reap sparingly, and whoever sows generously will also reap generously.*

(2 Corinthians 9:6 NIV)

God's Promises for Those Who...

572. *Give, and it will be given to you. A good measure, pressed down, shaken together and running over, will be poured into your lap. For with the measure you use, it will be measured to you.*   (Luke 6:38 NIV)

573. *God loves a cheerful giver.*
                    (2 Corinthians 9:7 NIV)

574. *A generous man will prosper; he who refreshes others will himself be refreshed.*
                    (Proverbs 11:25 NIV)

575. *God is able to make it up to you by giving you everything you need and more so that there will not only be enough for your own needs but plenty left over to give joyfully to others.*   (2 Corinthians 9:8 TLB)

576. *Honor the Lord by giving him the first part of all your income, and he will fill your barns with wheat and barley and overflow your wine vats with the finest wines.*   (Proverbs 3:9–10 TLB)

577. *"Bring the whole tithe into the storehouse, that there may be food in my house. Test me in this," says the LORD Almighty, "and see if I will not throw open the floodgates of heaven and pour out so much blessing that you will not have room enough for it."*
                    (Malachi 3:10 NIV)

578. *If you give to the poor, your needs will be supplied!* (Proverbs 28:27 TLB)

SUFFER FOR CHRIST

579. *If indeed we share in his sufferings...we may also share in his glory. I consider that our present sufferings are not worth comparing with the glory that will be revealed in us.* (Romans 8:17–18 NIV)

580. *God will tenderly comfort you when you undergo these same sufferings. He will give you the strength to endure.* (2 Corinthians 1:7 TLB)

581. *These troubles and sufferings of ours are, after all, quite small and won't last very long. Yet this short time of distress will result in God's richest blessing upon us forever and ever!* (2 Corinthians 4:17 TLB)

582. *If you suffer for doing good and you endure it, this is commendable before God.* (1 Peter 2:20 NIV)

583. *God...is using your sufferings to make you ready for his Kingdom, while at the same time he is preparing judgment and punishment for those who are hurting you.* (2 Thessalonians 1:5–6 TLB)

584. *The God of all grace, who called you to his eternal glory in Christ, after you have suffered a little while, will himself restore you and make you strong, firm and steadfast.*
(1 Peter 5:10 NIV)

585. *If you are insulted because of the name of Christ, you are blessed, for the Spirit of glory and of God rests on you.*
(1 Peter 4:14 NIV)

586. *I am comforted by this truth, that when we suffer and die for Christ it only means that we will begin living with him in heaven.*
(2 Timothy 2:11 TLB)

God's Promises for Those Who Are...

RIGHTEOUS

587. *The LORD loves the righteous.*
                                    (Psalm 146:8 NIV)

588. *He does not take his eyes off the righteous; he enthrones them with kings and exalts them forever.*   (Job 36:7 NIV)

589. *The righteous cry out, and the LORD hears them; he delivers them from all their troubles.*   (Psalm 34:17 NIV)

590. *The prospect of the righteous is joy....The way of the LORD is a refuge for the righteous.*   (Proverbs 10:28–29 NIV)

591. *The path of the righteous is like the first gleam of dawn, shining ever brighter till the full light of day.*   (Proverbs 4:18 NIV)

592. *The righteous stand firm forever....The righteous will never be uprooted.*
                              (Proverbs 10:25, 30 NIV)

593. *The desire of the righteous shall be granted.* (Proverbs 10:24 KJV)

594. *Those who receive God's abundant provision of grace and of the gift of righteousness reign in life through the one man, Jesus Christ.* (Romans 5:17 NIV)

595. *The righteous will shine like the sun in the kingdom of their Father.*
                              (Matthew 13:43 NIV)

596. *For surely, O LORD, you bless the righteous; you surround them with your favor as with a shield.* (Psalm 5:12 NIV)

GODLY

597. *The LORD has set apart the godly for himself; the LORD will hear when I call to him.*
                              (Psalm 4:3 NIV)

598. *The godly shall flourish like palm trees and grow tall as the cedars of Lebanon. For they are transplanted into the Lord's own garden and are under his personal care.* (Psalm 92:12–13 TLB)

599. *You bless the godly man, O Lord; you pro-tect him with your shield of love.*
(Psalm 5:12 TLB)

600. *The steps of good men are directed by the Lord. He delights in each step they take. If they fall it isn't fatal, for the Lord holds them with his hand.* (Psalm 37:23–24 TLB)

601. *God is good, and he loves goodness; the godly shall see his face.* (Psalm 11:7 TLB)

602. *Day by day the Lord observes the good deeds done by godly men, and gives them eternal rewards. He cares for them when times are hard; even in famine, they will have enough.* (Psalm 37:18–19 TLB)

603. *When a man's ways please the LORD, he maketh even his enemies to be at peace with him.* (Proverbs 16:7 KJV)

604. *Godliness with contentment is great gain.*
(1 Timothy 6:6 NIV)

605. *The godly are able to be generous with their gifts and loans to others, and their children are a blessing.* (Psalm 37:26 TLB)

606. *Godliness has value for all things, holding promise for both the present life and the life to come.* (1 Timothy 4:8 NIV)

DILIGENT WORKERS

607. *Do you know a hard-working man? He shall be successful and stand before kings!*
(Proverbs 22:29 TLB)

608. *The plans of the diligent lead to profit.*
(Proverbs 21:5 NIV)

609. *All hard work brings a profit, but mere talk leads only to poverty.*
(Proverbs 14:23 NIV)

610. *Wealth from gambling quickly disappears; wealth from hard work grows.*
(Proverbs 13:11 TLB)

611. *Don't work hard only when your master is watching and then shirk when he isn't looking; work hard and with gladness all the time, as though working for Christ, doing the will of God with all your hearts. Remember, the Lord will pay you for each good thing you do.* (Ephesians 6:6–8 TLB)

612. *Work hard so God can say to you, "Well done." Be a good workman, one who does not need to be ashamed when God examines your work.* (2 Timothy 2:15 TLB)

613. *Be ye strong therefore,...for your work shall be rewarded.* (2 Chronicles 15:7 KJV)

HONEST

614. *The LORD detests lying lips, but he delights in men who are truthful.*
(Proverbs 12:22 NIV)

615. *The man of integrity walks securely, but he who takes crooked paths will be found out.*
(Proverbs 10:9 NIV)

616. *Do you want a long, good life? Then watch your tongue! Keep your lips from lying.*
(Psalm 34:12–13 TLB)

617. *LORD, who may dwell in your sanctuary? Who may live on your holy hill? He whose walk is blameless and who does what is righteous, who speaks the truth from his heart and has no slander on his tongue.*
(Psalm 15:1–3 NIV)

618. *Who may stand before the Lord? Only those with pure hands and hearts, who do not practice dishonesty and lying. They will receive God's own goodness as their blessing from him, planted in their lives by God himself, their Savior.*
(Psalm 24:3–5 TLB)

619. *Truthful lips endure forever, but a lying tongue lasts only a moment.*
(Proverbs 12:19 NIV)

620. *Lies will get any man into trouble, but honesty is its own defense. Telling the truth gives a man great satisfaction.*
(Proverbs 12:13–14 TLB)

621. *All who are honest and fair, who reject making profit by fraud, who hold back their hands from taking bribes,...such as these shall dwell on high....Your eyes will see the King in his beauty and the highlands of heaven far away.*
(Isaiah 33:15–17 TLB)

FAITHFUL

622. *A faithful man will be richly blessed, but one eager to get rich will not go unpunished.* (Proverbs 28:20 NIV)

623. *His master replied, "Well done, good and faithful servant! You have been faithful with a few things; I will put you in charge of many things. Come and share your master's happiness!"* (Matthew 25:21 NIV)

624. *Let love and faithfulness never leave you; bind them around your neck, write them on the tablet of your heart. Then you will win favor and a good name in the sight of God and man.* (Proverbs 3:3–4 NIV)

625. *He that is faithful in that which is least is faithful also in much: and he that is unjust in the least is unjust also in much.*

(Luke 16:10 KJV)

626. *Love the LORD, all his saints! The LORD preserves the faithful, but the proud he pays back in full.*   (Psalm 31:23 NIV)

627. *Who then is the faithful and wise servant, whom the master has put in charge of the servants in his household to give them their food at the proper time? It will be good for that servant whose master finds him doing so when he returns. I tell you the truth, he will put him in charge of all his possessions.*   (Matthew 24:45–47 NIV)

628. *Remain faithful even when facing death and I will give you the crown of life—an unending, glorious future.*

(Revelation 2:10 TLB)